The Impossible Turned Possible

the Impossible
Turned
Possible

*How to Turn
Your Dreams
into Reality*

Carolyn
Hardy

NEW YORK

LONDON • NASHVILLE • MELBOURNE • VANCOUVER

The Impossible Turned Possible

How to Turn Your Dreams Into Reality

© 2021 Carolyn Hardy

Published in New York, New York, by Morgan James Publishing. Morgan James is a trademark of Morgan James, LLC. www.MorganJamesPublishing.com

ISBN 9781631952586 paperback
ISBN 9781631952593 eBook
Library of Congress Control Number: 2020940200

Cover Design by:
Rachel Lopez
www.r2cdesign.com

Interior Design by:
Christopher Kirk
www.GFSstudio.com

Morgan James is a proud partner of Habitat for Humanity Peninsula and Greater Williamsburg. Partners in building since 2006.

Get involved today! Visit
MorganJamesPublishing.com/giving-back

TABLE OF CONTENTS

INTRODUCTION

Why should you read *The Impossible Turned Possible*?

We all know people who dreamed of a different life ... but they wake up forty years later still in the same place. The conversation usually goes something like this: *After graduating from high school, I planned to be a teacher or nurse, but life has a way of taking you in a different direction. Therefore, my dreams will never happen.* Or maybe it's something like this: *I can't exercise because I have children. I want the next promotion in my department, but I don't think my boss likes me. She resents me because it's not my job to make her look good.*

This mindset—this fixed mindset that says *I have no control of my life* is your worst enemy. It holds you back, which is making you unhappy. You picked up this little book because something in your life feels impossible, feels out of your control.

You are in the right place. *The Impossible Turned Possible* will transform your attitude about change and winning.

Dr. Martin Luther King Jr. said, "Take the first step in faith. You don't have to see the whole staircase, just take that first step."

We all resist change. For most of us, the first step toward change is always the hardest. We find comfort in normalcy. And the bigger the change, the harder the first step is. We are frightened by not knowing the outcome of the change. We doubt ourselves, and we overthink. But once the ice is broken by the first step taken, the rest can fall into place more easily.[1]

---

1   https://blogs.rochester.edu/
      thegreendandelion/2018/01/take-the-first-step/

Sustainable change requires behavior change to be the first step. This change in your behavior, such as belief in yourself or ridding yourself of excuses, is crucial for achieving your long-term goals. We all have aspirations, things we know we can do better, but where do you start? Old habits are hard to break—but not impossible. After taking the first step, every small change toward your goal will lead to another. Every positive action with a positive outcome builds confidence, which is the beginning of your transformation.

It's amazing how human nature gives the fear of failure more power than the rewards of success. Dreamers dream without taking action because of their fear, but people of action find a way to achieve outcomes they desire. The stories in *The Impossible Turned Possible* will inspire you and challenge you to reimagine your life as well as provide a road map to guide you on your journey.

But I must caution you: Success is as addictive as failure. Once you take that first step, it is harder to go back to an easier way.

This book is your secret weapon to learn how to accomplish your goals. My hope is that you replace old habits of doing nothing with new structured habits, building your confidence to win. Good luck on your journey to becoming a winner—your new normal.

Let's take the first step to reimagining the awesome you, the first of many firsts for you on the way to achieving the life you deserve.

"Impossible is just a big word thrown around by small men who find it easier to live in the world they've been given than to explore the power they have to change it. Impossible is not a fact. It's an opinion. Impossible is not a declaration. It's a dare. Impossible is potential. Impossible is temporary. Impossible is nothing."
—**Muhammad Ali**, American professional boxer, activist, and philanthropist

ACKNOWLEDGMENTS

Everyone loves a winner, and everyone wants to be a winner. We all love to see underdogs win. My target audience for this book is anyone who pursued a goal but stopped before getting started. I have seen too many people give up without trying. Most heroes in my life were everyday person who wanted to help others achieve a better outcome requiring nothing in return. I want to thank these silent heroes who helped me and many others believe they could turn the Impossible to Possible.

My life started in such poverty that the world

classified my family as losers or a drain on society. Therefore, what did I have to lose chasing the impossible? My advantage was my great parents, Lois and Sidney Chism. My dad's captivating personality taught us that a great personality opens doors. My elegant, classy mom was a visionary who taught her children that your only limitation is you. She taught us selfless leadership and inspired us to continually learn. Mom dreamed big and placed her life's mistakes on center stage to help her children learn from the past while pursuing excellence and ambition. My mother's life work was motivating and encouraging her children while challenging us to achieve our personal best. This lady with an eleventh-grade education inspired future generations by teaching the value of an education. My mom deserves the Freedom Award since education is the key to freedom.

Any significant accomplishments in life require great partners. My partner, soulmate, and spouse, Marino Hardy, has shown enduring respect and steadfast support of my journey. When we met as teenagers, he realized I was unique, and it didn't frighten him. Instead of being scared away, he signed up for a lifetime of change and challenges. My other great partners are our wonderful children: Jennifer, Whitney and Christopher. Thank you for your love, friendship and support of my endless pursuit of a different future. They now know my goal was to create a better world for them. Thank you for your love and support of my never-ending adventures.

As the seventh of sixteen children, my siblings are my village. They invested mentally, emotionally and financially in my accomplishments. My supportive brothers and sisters cultivated greatness in me at an early age. They sacrificed personally for my college education and tireless assistance in raising my three amazing children. We are extremely close siblings. At times, I wonder if my in-laws ever get feed up with our closeness. If we attend an event without a seating chart, we migrate to each other and forget about others since all we need for fun is each other's company. We must be strategically separated to focus on others or the occasion. Whenever my family is in the house, I am at the right place at the right time. My village is my life. Thank you for your love, support and guidance.

A great company requires unselfish support and dedication. I was blessed with the support of two dedicated individuals, Bernadette Fuller and Phil Potts. We worked sixteen-hour days sometimes seven days a week. Our roles included cleaning toilets, lawn care, repairing equipment, developing quality systems, engaging our team, selling, and developing our business strategies. This amazing team was loyal, dependable and passionate. The success of Hardy Bottling was our success. Hardy Bottling had many great experiences but the most valuable was the team's mutual respect and loyalty creating a bond for life.

In life, everyone is looking for a break or an opportunity to give them a chance. Oprah Winfrey, actress, author, TV personality said, "The most important journey of our lives doesn't necessarily involve climbing the highest peak or trekking around the world. The biggest adventure you can ever take is to live the life of your dreams." This team allowed me to live the life of my dreams. These relationships were and are not only priceless but create a force of nature that takes on challenges to improve the lives of others in the community. I stand on the shoulders of these giants in my life. Now, I seek ways like writing *The Impossible Turned Possible* to create many giants for generations to come.

CHAPTER 1

When I was eight years old, our home burned down.

My mother and seven of her fifteen children (two died in early childhood) were sitting in the living room watching TV while two babies slept in the bedroom.

To this day, I don't remember what motivated me to walk into the kitchen. As I opened the door, flames burst through the doorway. The entire rear of the house was engulfed in fire and smoke. I screamed, causing my mother to spring into action. She instructed her kids, ages four to ten, to

1

exit the house as she retrieved her babies from the crib. My siblings and I were standing outside in absolute fear. The lady who made our life possible was running back into the blaze.

Within minutes, she re-appeared amidst the smoke, saving my brother and sister. She fell to the ground with singed hair and eyebrows. One baby suffered moderate burns and the other remained unscathed. The house was reduced to ashes by the time fire trucks arrived. Those embers glow as vivid in my mind today as the day I first witnessed my mother turn the impossible to possible.

When I think about the challenges I face, both past and present, the achievements and victories that appeared out of my grasp, I remember the bravery my mom displayed that night and realize my challenges hardly compare. Through any challenges I face, I strive to bring the same energy my mother mustered for her children. Mom had to think quickly and logically in a time of crisis; her babies would not have survived without her quick action and determination. Many lives depended on her leadership during the fire, and she turned the impossible to possible.

Despite the fire department's insistence on avoiding a burning building, Mom believed saving her babies was possible. She had no one telling her she would not be successful. The key to her success was her blind determination to save her children's lives. At no point did she believe her goal to be impossible.

In life, everything is not of equal importance; prioritization is key. She never said, "We lost everything." She accomplished the impossible by saving what was important. This was my first encounter with the impossible turned possible. I still become emotional every time I think about it. The incident is imprinted in my mind and heart forever.

PLANNING THE JOURNEY

According to research from the U.S. Chamber of Commerce, only 3 percent of adult citizens in the United States take the time and put in the effort to plan for the future, but this 3 percent accomplishes five to ten times more in their lifetimes than the other 97 percent. Most people spend more time planning their vacations than planning their financial investments because vacation is seen as a short-term escape from the day-to-day reality while financial investments represent more meaningful change in your life—long-term escape, which can change your family's quality of life. Individuals who take the time to determine what they want to achieve and develop a plan are much more likely to accomplish their goals than those who leave their lives to chance. There is magic and power in planning.

Larry Winget, author and speaker, said, "Nobody ever wrote down a plan to be broke, fat, lazy, or stupid. Those things are what happen when you don't have a plan."

Many people dream of winning the lottery. They dream about how they will spend the money to reach the goals they have not accomplished, things like purchasing a home, career aspirations, entrepreneurship, or other life-changing goals. But the conversation ends with excuses about why they are not able to achieve those goals without a chance win like the lottery. They believe success is reserved for extraordinary people. They believe success is out of reach. The goal of this book is to demonstrate how planning is key to achieving your goals and the life you deserve—without winning the lottery.

GOAL SETTING: SET SMART GOALS

The benefit of setting a goal and a subsequent plan is it becomes the roadmap for your journey. It keeps you on course even when life offers you new opportunities or challenges. By setting a goal and developing your plan to reach it, you focus on your choices. This gives you the mindset of having control over your life so you can continue to make choices on the way.

For example, a vacation plan makes your journey more pleasurable. You need to know where you are going and how you will get there. Detailed preparation decreases the risk of things going wrong with your journey. It's the same with goal setting and planning—planning *increases the pos-*

sibility that your life will go in the right direction, the direction you want it to go.

Now that you know why goal setting and planning are critical for your outcome, let's go over where to start. I follow a five-step approach best summarized by Andrew Farrelly in a 2017 article entitled "Get Real SMART: Setting Goals—Well":

1. Make Sure Your Goals are SMART: specific, measureable, attainable, relevant, and time specific. I also live my life by the KISS theory: keep it simple stupid. SMART is a simple guideline for setting goals anyone can follow.

> **Specific:** Your goal is clearly defined. For example, "I want to lose weight" is vague. Instead, "I want to lose thirty pounds" is specific or "I want to graduate by 2019."

> **Measurable:** Quantify your goal so you know when it's achieved. Start by being specific as we discussed above. Losing weight is good but stating your specific goal will be more moti-

vational. The thirty-pound weight loss or the year 2019 is measurable.

Attainable: Set a stretch goal that challenges you while making it realistic based upon your capabilities within your control. An unattainable goal may frustrate you and set you up for failure.

Relevant: Your goals help you achieve the life you deserve or achieve plans for your life. Therefore, it is important not only understand what your goals are but why they are important to you and your family. This will be your motivation to follow your plan.

Time Specific: Set a deadline (date) by which your goal will be achieved. A goal of losing thirty pounds without a date does not create a sense of urgency. Losing thirty pounds in eighteen months with interim weight loss at key milestones helps you monitor and measure your progress.

2. Set Milestones

The due date for a goal is typically far away. Many people put off starting until the first milestone approaches. Therefore, look at the project and set milestones based upon the accomplishment of anything significant. For example, losing weight may require a monthly weight loss goal since new habits are needed to stay on target. In the case of savings, if you want to save $100,000 and plan to save $2,000 per month, review the dollar amount saved monthly. This approach helps you monitor and measure your progress. Additionally, it helps you get back on target without significant time lapse if you do fall off the wagon for a little while.

3. Develop Action Steps to Reach Your Goals

List specific actions needed to reach big goals within the timeframe you decided on. In the case of weight loss, you may want to hire a personal trainer. Set a goal with the support of the trainer. Another key action could be to meet with a nutritionist to change your dietary habits. You may have a walking goal that gets increasingly aggressive over time. You may decide to run or walk a marathon after year one. These activities are all necessary to achieve the thirty-pound weight loss and create good habits to maintain your new weight.

4. Put Your Actions into a Schedule

Develop a plan to get started. The first task will be the hardest as the first step but keep your eye on the prize (accomplishing your goal). It can be as simple as starting to walk each day. Next could be a call to a personal trainer and nutritionist to set up your first meetings to understand what is involved in the journey and lay to rest fears of the unknown. This first step will get you excited. Even if you start with baby steps, any action builds confidence and momentum.

5. Monitor Progress

Follow your schedule and do the daily tasks you've planned. Develop a plan that allows you to be consistent so your actions become new habits. This is critical to achieving your plan since you are trying to create a new norm for yourself. Your personal progress report will keep you motivated and create accountability to keep you on target. Remember: What gets measured gets done. I would recommend you maintain a log of your accomplishments and results. Set aside time every month to review your progress and make adjustments if necessary.

These five steps help me do the impossible. They will help you set your goals and develop a supporting detailed plan. The steps in the plan keep me focused on accomplishing my goals and the process brought clarity to my goals and realistic strategies to achieve them. Remember: A goal without a plan will remain an impossible dream. Think about what you want to accomplish in life. Then begin your journey to the life you deserve.

CHAPTER 2

MY JOURNEY

Before sharing my journey of achieving lofty goals, I need to share the dark side of success. I want you to understand that you will experience a dark side. The greater the goal and the more successful you become, the ever darker it gets. I confess, I made mistakes. I had many sleepless nights after setbacks or unfair situations. But when people ask what happened after those setbacks, I tell them I went to bed and when I woke up, it was a new day. A new day brings a fresh outlook, a refreshed attitude, and more determination. The obstacles caused setbacks to my goals, not a fire. I learned lessons from each obstacle, which made me a stronger person.

Life is a rose garden filled with pebbles and thorns. The thorns represent problems with achieving my goals. They made success feel out of reach. The key to my success was how I managed those obstacles or thorns. At no point did I give up on my goal. I tripped, stumbled, and fell on my face, but I always get back up. Before you start your journey to the life you deserve, accept you will have similar obstacles. Anticipate problems.

Now you are ready to start learning about achieving lofty or impossible goals.

THE POVERTY CYCLE

The U. S. Department of Education reports that students from sixteen to twenty-four years old from low-income families are seven times more likely to drop out than their more well-off peers. Studies show that college graduates earn significantly more money throughout their lifetime than those with only high school education. According to a national report by the State Higher Education Executive Officers (sheeo.org), high school graduates earn an average of almost $30,000 per year. Graduates with a bachelor's degree earn an average of just over $50,000 a year. And those with a higher-level degree (master's, doctorate, or professional) average nearly $70,000 per year. This translates to a significant earnings gap over the course of one's life.

The Federal Reserve Board's Survey of Consumer Finances reports that the more education you receive, the higher your chance of becoming a millionaire across all races. The survey predicts a 37 percent probability that a White person with a master's degree becomes a millionaire. That 37 percent looks incredibly high compared to the low probability for Hispanics and Blacks to become millionaires even with a master's degree. You'd think that by the time you get to the master's level of education that the people and institutions you hang around with would provide very similar financial and career opportunities for all races. But with Blacks who have earned master's degrees only having a 7 percent chance of becoming a million-aire compared to a 37 percent chance for Whites, something seems very wrong.

My mother, Lois Chism, recognized the need to break her family's poverty cycle. In high school, she set a goal of earning a college education. Instead, she married before finishing high school and immediately started her family. It deterred her dream. As a result, she redefined her goal with a loftier one. She dreamed of higher education for all of her children.

My mother was a great leader. She was a dream maker, not a dream slayer. She managed a team of sixteen people: her family. She led by example and emphasized education and skills as means to build the dreams of her family members. She wanted us to see the good in everyone we came into contact with. Even after someone would say or do some-thing awful, she would tell us, "Everybody has a little good in them and a little bad." She taught us to be empathetic and optimistic, to work hard and to show up. It was her life's journey to celebrate each of us for our unique talents and personalities.

BREAKING THE CYCLE

My mother understood that life has many cycles. The focus for her children was disrupting the poverty cycle and encouraging the success cycle. Poverty and wealth are cycles that pass from generation to generation. Many people have a mindset that says: It is impossible to accomplish a level of success that frees me from the poverty cycle. "If you do not like something, change it. If you can't change it, change your attitude. Don't complain," said Maya Angelou, famous writer and poet.

My mother embodied Maya Angelou's words as she cultivated her children's lives. She taught us not to complain while planning for a different life. She recognized a quality education could break the poverty cycle of her family. Therefore, she set a goal for each of her children to graduate either college or trade school. This accomplishment would ensure her children earned a living wage. And this ambitious education goal required a detailed plan.

Her plan required her children to be great students so they could earn scholarships. Every night, homework was a priority—not chores. The plan assigned older siblings to tutor younger siblings. It was the older sibling's responsibility to assist with the younger children's assignments. She measured our success by our report cards. The report cards were used to monitor progress and establish new goals. Grades were not allowed to decline. She taught us to be confident in our ability to achieve excellence.

As a maid for a doctor's family, my mother saw the doctor's children wanted to be a successful doctor like their father. My mother's fear was that her children would adopt her position as a maid as their role model. Therefore, her plan also required exposing her children to professionals to act as alternative role models. She decided her oldest daughter and son would become the family's role models. She did everything possible to ensure Juanita's success. As a result, Juanita was the first to graduate college in our family and became a teacher. My mother and the entire family were extremely proud of her accomplishment. Her education and subsequent teaching job immediately lifted her from poverty. My siblings and I saw firsthand the value of a college education. It was not a question of *if* we were going to college; instead, it was a question of how fast we could start. We attended summer school, took extra classes, and studied hard to graduate high school early. This motivated us to start our careers as soon as possible.

My mother's second role model was my brother, Scnear. My mother sent him to trade school to become a car mechanic. After graduation, he learned the pay was below a living wage. Therefore, she adjusted her goal of obtaining a skill that paid a living wage. Subsequently he became a union painter, which immediately lifted him out of poverty.

Now my mother's family had two career options as role models for success with an understanding of which careers to avoid.

She had many setbacks to accomplishing her goal, such as competing with providing basic needs. In college, we worked part-time, applied for scholarships and grants, and lived at home. We understood our strengths were great work ethic, determination, and being driven. The real threat was disappointing our mom, which was not going to happen. Her confidence in our ability to excel provided the fuel for us to face and survive many negative situations. She was both cheerleader and drill sergeant.

I was born in poverty. I lived below the poverty line my entire childhood. However, poverty did not define me. Instead, I was defined by my mother's goal of her children earning a higher education. Her six girls graduated college and eight sons completed high school, some completing college and all completing trade schools as planned. Society believes a black woman with sixteen children is destined for public assistance. My mother's impossible was her goal of breaking the poverty cycle through higher education. She proved it is possible for children raised in poverty to achieve higher education, successful careers, and financial independence.

As the survey shows, statistics were against Mom's plan for her children, but with a great plan and determination, she defied statistics. Her life's work was her children's exodus from poverty, which defied the norm. She taught us values each day and became the best role model for her children. She believed parents and leaders must represent the values they want their children or employees to embrace.

Statistics say I should have remained in poverty. No one shared these statistics with me, so I did not know I was supposed to fail. Society must stop telling kids in poverty they have limited opportunity to change their situation. We must instead share words of encouragement and hope. We must believe all kids can gain higher education, regardless of their current situation. Society should provide hope, not place a cloud over those born in unfortunate situations. Let's not reinforce statistics with our actions. Instead, let's encourage children to achieve a level of education that helps them achieve their personal best. With that mindset, I believe we can create new statistics.

Thank you, Mom, for defying the odds and making your family the new statistic.

CHAPTER 3

JOURNEY TO FINANCIAL FREEDOM

Kyle Maynard is a speaker, author, and mixed martial arts athlete known for becoming the first quadruple amputee to ascend Mount Kilimanjaro with the aid of prosthetics. Maynard was born with no arms or legs but climbed 19,341 feet and crawled twenty-five miles over twelve days to reach the summit. Maynard's story is a great example of how tasks that seem overwhelming or impossible can be accomplished if we break them down into manageable steps.

As I've said, my life's journey began in extreme poverty. As a four-year-old, I was trained to scavenge through dumpsters for food that was discarded by the grocery store to help my family survive. Each summer, I went to the park for free lunches and waited until everyone was served to bring any surplus food home. I slept on a mattress on the floor with four siblings until the age of fifteen. Even in poverty, Mom taught us to dream big. Society says it would be impossible for someone of my socioeconomic background to save a million dollars. Many would say my dreams and ambitions were good examples of a pipe dream. Imagine how difficult it is for people in situations like mine to envision themselves outside of their normal environment with the world telling them their dreams are impossible.

SETTING A HIGH BAR

At twenty-two, I set a high goal for myself. I planned on becoming a millionaire by the age of forty. I had lived my entire childhood in poverty. If I had discussed my goal with anyone, many would have considered this goal to be impossible; they would have discouraged rather than encouraged me. My exposure to millionaires was limited since I had never met one. Now, when I reflect on becoming a millionaire, I realize my real desire was financial security.

Setting this lofty goal was the first step in my achieving an unconventional and unrealistic goal. I knew a million dollars was out of reach for someone with limited access to opportunities. The key steps in my plan required me to expand my education and develop a saving strategy, discipline, and creative thinking relative to earning and spending. I did not fear failure. Some fear of risk is beneficial if it causes you to anticipate potential problems, but being paralyzed by risk and fear is counterproductive because it prevents action. At twenty-two, I had the advantage of youth. I knew I could try again if I was unsuccessful.

This journey began with communication and collaboration with my husband, Marino. We discussed the goal and the required sacrifices. We agreed to a strong partnership, working as a team, or we would fail. This financial goal required new skills. I enrolled in investment, finance, and real estate classes at the University of Memphis. I opened a brokerage account to make small stock purchases to test my knowledge. I studied each company's proxy materials, annual reports, and any information about their growth plans to identify undervalued stocks before making an investment. After achieving a set return, I would sell the stock. This helped me to understand the stock market while establishing another income stream.

Armed with my newfound education, I developed a diversified investment plan. The plan required my husband and I to start doing new things, forming new habits. We limited our living expenses to a single paycheck. We saved 100 percent of the other paycheck. We maximized our 401K contributions since 401K investments would yield a high return from our employers' 50 percent matching program. I invested personal savings in high growth mutual funds. We reduced tax liability by maximizing contributions to our IRAs. As we monitored our progress each month, each year of high savings and great yields brought a million-dollar dream closer to possible.

Our plan also required us to stop doing some things to reduce expenses. We eliminated costs like cable and identified creative ways to reduce costs in every category. We installed thermostat controllers to reduce energy cost. The entire family shopped for deals. The children and I were organized coupon clippers. My son had a coupon wallet. The children would make their Christmas lists by cutting out the picture of the items, finding a coupon, and identifying the store with the best prices.

The plan included investments in our children's education as well. Our vacations were investments in cultural education. We hired tutors to ensure they excelled academically. Education was an important part of our family's culture and our plan. This earned each of our children scholarships. Now my children are on their way to setting their own lofty goals.

Let's revisit the statistics. The Federal Reserve survey reported only 7 percent of minorities with a master's degree become millionaires. I was lucky I was never told my likelihood of achieving this goal was so low. Instead, I accomplished this impossible financial goal at the age of thirty-seven—three years ahead of schedule.

What happens when a great plan comes together? What is the value of planning to achieve a lofty goal?

I became a millionaire one dollar at a time, using small steps and a solid plan.

CHAPTER 4

JOURNEY FROM POVERTY TO FOUNDER

After achieving my dream of financial stability, I decided it was time for a change in my career. In 2006, I decided to purchase Coors Brewing Company's facility and assets in Memphis, Tennessee. A fifteen-million-dollar loan was required to purchase the brewery and its assets and provide working capital. Once again, a detailed plan was required—this time for business.

Coors's assets would allow for the production of most liquid beverages and package types. Memphis's central location optimized transportation costs. This contract beverage facility had the capability to support the beverage industry growth in the United States.

The plan required extensive research into the beverage industry. The research identified beverage growth trends by type of beverage. We mapped all contract beverage companies in the U.S. and used the information for financial projections, marketing plans, and sales strategies. This research helped me develop a very effective business plan to guide my new business. It was also used to help financial institutions and other potential investors understand the business opportunity.

As part of my research, I interviewed other business owners to identify threats and opportunities for a new business venture. A new business owner must have great credit to secure loans and a line of credit. Many new business owners must initially guarantee credit with vendors. Fortunately, I had great credit with significant savings. We used personal savings for 20 percent of the loan and planned to borrow the fifteen million dollars.

My plan's action steps required the plan to be evaluated by a seasoned professional. I chose John Malmo, founder of Archer Malmo advertising. I asked him to evaluate my marketing plan and business strategy.

In preparation for this meeting, I read John's book, *Monkey is King* and updated my business plan to incorporate advice from his book. In the meeting with John, I presented my short- and long-term strategies. I highlighted where my plan was consistent with recommendations from his book. I had integrated the easy advice from John's book into my business plan. Therefore, the meeting inspired John to not only validate my plan but also provide new recommendations to improve the plan. He was impressed with my short-term plan to guide the company to financial stability. We focused most of our discussion on the first three years since this is the timeframe when most new businesses succeed or fail.

My financial plan was very detailed. I understood that borrowing fifteen million dollars was not going to be easy. Therefore, I worked multiple channels to apply for funds to meet the Coors contract timeline. After presenting to every major financial institution and many private investors in Memphis, everyone rejected me. They would not take the risk. A former Merrill Lynch banker called me and said, "Carolyn, the banks will not loan you money. They will keep changing the requirements." This had been my experience for months. So, he recommended a hard moneylender named Guerry Moore from Oklahoma.

I also interviewed potential partners, but they would only agree to invest if they had a controlling interest. I was told to avoid investors who want 51 percent ownership. Since I invested the initial capital, I required my partners to own 49 percent or less. My rule was to advise potential investors early in the meeting that I was not giving up control. This saved everyone time and frustration.

The banks' loan processes were frustrating, intimidating, and eye-opening. Many banks told me they wanted to do a big deal with a black female. I said, "Great, this is a big deal, and I am a black female." After the banks' requirements continued to change, I realized they were seeking a positive way to let me down. I said to myself, "If the banks wanted to make a substantial loan to a black female in Memphis who could make a 20 percent personal investment, the last time I checked, Oprah does not need a loan or live in Memphis. I'm right here!"

I finally met with the hard moneylender, Guerry Moore. After reviewing my business plan, he said he could place the loan. I completed my loan with the hard moneylender in thirty days. I could not borrow the low-interest TVA or 504B funds, which require a bank loan. This hard money group had never made a fifteen-million-dollar loan to a black woman.

Five years after the loan, I asked Guerry if I had made him more money than his other clients. He said this was the best return of his career. It was the best return in my career as well.

Success was possible because I followed Mom's advice. Mom taught us to respect our elders and those with experience in an area we are seeking knowledge. She said, "Be fearless by asking for help since the worst they can say is 'no.' Their knowledge can contribute to your success."

My education provided the skills to perform the research and develop a detailed business plan. The action steps guided me while ensuring compliance with Coors's sales agreement timeline. I used my network to find advisors with the skills and experience I needed to learn to achieve my goals. Success is rarely achieved as a solo act.

As a result of a thorough business plan, confidence in my ability and competence helped me to secure a loan. My lenders enjoyed a new experience loaning money to a black woman to start Hardy Bottling. I became the first African American female in the nation to own a major brewery.

Listening is an art, and successful execution is the finished portrait. I knew that this was only the beginning.

CHAPTER 5

JOURNEY INTERRUPTED BY HEALTH CRISIS

Henry Ford, founder of Ford Motor Company, said, "Whether you think you can, or you think you can't—you're right." This quote emphasizes how much attitude determines your success or failure. This is true whether your attitude is about career, business, or health.

"Your outlook—having a sense of optimism and purpose—seems to be predictive of health outcomes," says Dr. Laura Kubzansky, professor of social and behavioral sciences at Harvard. She said that the vitality of a life is characterized by enthusiasm, hopefulness, engagement, and the ability to face life's stresses with emotional balance. She found that emotional vitality is associated with a substantially reduced risk of both heart attack and stroke.

Examples of your outlook include your basic attitude about life. Do you look forward to the next week? Do you feel younger than your age? Do you have a sense of purpose? If so, you may already have reduced your risk of degenerative diseases and may even add years to your life.

I was at the hairdresser when I received a call from my doctor after 5 p.m., which was unusual. She said, "Carolyn, I have bad news. Your mammogram came back showing a lump." The joy and freedom from buying the brewery was short-lived. This call from my doctor caught me off guard.

I didn't react because I was in shock. My mind was reeling. I had invested 50 percent of my family's wealth in this company. I had two children in high school planning to attend college. My family could not operate this business without me. It was my vision, experience, and business plan we were executing. My mind was screaming, "What have I gotten my family into? If I do not recover, they will suffer because of my ambition."

The only thing I knew to do was prepare for recovery and live.

My doctor said there was no way to know the severity of the lump. But she also said, "Carolyn, I need to you to take this seriously and make this procedure a priority."

Even though there was no way of knowing the outcome, the doctor didn't want to wait to make a diagnosis because an early diagnosis correlates with a better prognosis. She explained, "I know you are under a lot of pressure with your new company, but this is more than a distraction."

We scheduled a biopsy, and my results would be available in three weeks.

The first week, I was in survival mode. My goal was simple: Survive the health crisis while not going bankrupt during recovery. My original business plan required building a team that could operate the business in my absence. I had assembled a management team of people I had worked with in the past. But the team was starting three months later. I asked them to start immediately. These managers were my trusted allies and confidantes; they had my back. When I confidentially shared my diagnosis with them, they gave their two-week notices that same day and came on board.

Three weeks later, I received results no one wants to hear. It was cancer.

The next month I had a lumpectomy. But the cancer had metastasized. Therefore, the lumpectomy did not remove the cancer. The best chance of beating the cancer required a mastectomy.

A month after the mastectomy, I had surgery to place a port catheter in my chest to receive chemotherapy. A month later, the catheter was defective, and I was back in surgery. I had surgery every month from October through January. I did all of this while starting a new company.

My plan was to hire the best specialists and follow their advice to treat my cancer. My plan also required me to increase delegation to the management team. This actually increased the skillset of the entire team. My plan included using the chemo sessions as my quiet time for creative thinking and reflection. This also became my time to work on email and other business writing. My treatment team formulated my chemotherapeutic cocktail to slow me down and make me sleep. I told the nurse I would not sleep, which I did not. They finally gave up and removed the Benadryl from my medication.

Mentally, I believed, "God did not bring me this far to die." I maintained a positive attitude. My chief concern was always my family. I did not want them to worry about my fight. At work, my cancer was never discussed because I was terrified the lenders would recall their loan if I appeared physically weak.

After three years of fighting, my doctor said the cancer was in remission; I had won. And I have the scars to prove it! I would not wish this difficult time on anyone, but I became a stronger person with a more capable team from it.

Why was I successful?

First, my new business had a succession plan. A company is not one person; instead, it is a team. The leadership had the experience and skills to manage the business. This gave me peace of mind during my recovery. This type of plan requires both confidence in your team and a strong relationship with your team. My health crisis journey required planning. The steps in the plans required a willing and loyal leadership team, supportive family, faith in God, a positive attitude, and determination. Also, my goal of living was reflected in my positive attitude and adherence to the doctor's instructions.

My realistic business plan borrowed sufficient funds to manage the business for at least two years without a profit. We wanted to earn a profit in year one, but I am a realist. This took the pressure off raising funds during recovery.

My primary threat would have been a bad outcome from the cancer. My contingent action would have been to sell the assets to repay the loans.

When I think about this health crisis, I think about Dr. Laura Kubzansky's study about the effects a positive perspective has on health. During my health crisis, my attitude was that I would survive this since God did not bring me this far to fail. Each day, I also practiced the following:

- Recognize something positive each day.
- In a tough situation, list what went right as well as what went wrong.
- Congratulate yourself on small wins; tell yourself you are a winner.
- Spend time understanding your strengths and tell yourself how awesome you are.
- Dress to help your attitude; dress good, feel good.
- Set attainable goals versus setting yourself up for failure.
- Recognize and practice small acts of kindness daily; complement others.
- Do activities that take your mind off problems.

My mother taught us to look our best every day, be physically fit, and do everything in moderation. My doctor was amazed at the speed of my recovery. A week after surgery, he said I looked healthier than his staff. My personal positive attitude was that I refused to let a little thing like cancer impede my destiny.

And it worked.

CONCLUSION

A major problem today is there are too many excuses for why we cannot succeed. Great leaders do not accept excuses. What I have learned in the last thirty years is that *excuses* are the *food* that feeds *failure*. As leaders, we must encourage our team members to seek solutions. A problem or crisis is a great opportunity to show how exceptional you are by turning the impossible to possible.

Too many people believe education and success are reserved for extraordinary people, not those in poverty. The truth is, we all have an opportunity to achieve greatness. We all know people who claim to be lucky by being in the right place at the right time. They appear to be successful without lifting a finger. This is a myth. You must put in the work. The reality is, there are no overnight success stories.

On July 20, 1969, the Apollo 11 spacecraft landed on the moon with Neil Armstrong, the first human to walk on the moon. This was an accomplishment of epic proportions. What can we, as leaders, learn from the Apollo project? Starting in 1961, over nine years before the historic day, President John F. Kennedy set a big, lofty goal that defied the imagination of most Americans because it had never been done.

A young girl lives her entire childhood in poverty, learns from the age of four how to secure food for the family. Long before Uber and Lift, she runs errands for the neighborhood for a fee. She understands the free lunch programs in the city parks to subsidize the family's food in order to survive. Instead of complaining about her family's affairs, she dreams big about another life. Using her mom's wisdom and her college education, she defies society's statistics. Setting big, lofty goals with the five-step plan defies odds that were about as out of reach as placing a man on the moon. She understands that dreaming is free but achievement requires setting goals and developing a plan.

Carolyn would tell you that it was hard, risky, and challenging. She would also tell you that achieving a lofty goal is rewarding.

Few goals are bigger than landing a man on the moon. This goal was set before any American had even orbited the earth; yet, just seven days after we first launched a man into space, President Kennedy called his shot. He was ridiculed by many for setting this impossible goal.

Yet, it was achieved.

You will never reach an impossible goal if you don't set one. And if you set the goal too low, you may reach it, but you will never achieve what you really want. Dream it, plan it, and, most importantly, do it.

Before you know it, you will achieve your own moon landing or, as I like to say, your impossible turned possible.

CAROLYN CHISM HARDY

*Building Pathways
to Re-imagine Your Life*

Carolyn Chism Hardy is taking women and minority business by storm. She is a fearless innovator of change, moving forward in commercial real estate development and as a distributor, exporter, author, and philanthropist. She is a trailblazer whose accomplishments in non-traditional jobs, business triumphs, and entrepreneurial achievements are unequalled by women and Blacks. Hardy operates on the forefront of business evolution as she uses innovation, creative ideas, and networks to roll out the next generation of ideas.

Carolyn grew up in extreme poverty, moving thirteen times by the age of twelve. She understood that the simple human needs such as food, clothing, and shelter were many times beyond her family's reach. As a child, she took every opportunity to help the family survive versus worrying about what she did not have. She credits her parents, struggles to survive, and her refusal to be a statistic or stereotyped as her fuel to achieve the impossible.

Carolyn began her career at the J. M. Smucker Company, successfully managing the finance, quality, and human resources departments before becoming the first African American female plant manager. After a successful career at Smucker's, she served as vice president of services at Honeywell-POMS Corporation where she was responsible for domestic and international software implementation. She then joined Coors Brewing Company and became the first African American female vice president and general manager of a major brewery.

As the founder and CEO of Chism Hardy Investments, Hardy is a job creator, innovator, and philanthropist. A passionate and determined investor, she purchased a former Coors Brewery in 2006 and started Hardy Bottling Company, which she sold in 2011. In 2012, she stepped up her investment in the neighborhood where she had worked her entire career. She invested over five million dollars building a new grain system to export grain and expanding her commercial leasing holdings. This grain expansion with her daughters, Jennifer and Whitney, leveraged the Memphis location to create jobs in a sector that is not only right for Memphis, but is also great for farmers in Tennessee, Arkansas, and Mississippi. Her vision: to build a unique Memphis-based supply chain management company. Her pathway: strong partnerships, proper capitalization, and first-to-market solutions. "I want to be the proof women and minorities have the skills and ability to build a significant company while demonstrating that women- and minority-owned businesses can compete," she says.

Her words of guidance: "Test your boundaries. Test your resilience. Test your capacity. Be the best version of yourself, and connect with your audiences." As an experienced businessperson, insignificant challenges and temporary obstacles seldom distract her. Hardy stays focused and keeps on pushing regardless of the size of the mountain. As a published author, her goal is to reach a broader audience to teach others how she's managed to move mountains.

A devoted philanthropist, Hardy is a founding member of Philanthropic Black Women and a board member of Federal Reserve of St. Louis, Tennessee Lottery, Tennessee Leadership Business Council, Methodist Le Bonheur Hospital, Greater Memphis Chamber, SCORE, and many others. Her vision is to build a vibrant community that is inclusive to increase prosperity for all.

Carolyn is engaged in Memphis's "rebirth" and industry growth through her support of the growth in skilled manufacturing jobs. As one of the founders of Southwest Industrial Readiness program, thousands of unemployed and under-employed Memphians have been trained and have secured jobs that pay a living wage and include benefits. Carolyn's primary objective is to support a greater Memphis by promoting growth and prosperity for all people.

"Every time the needle moves in Memphis, I work to ensure the needle moves for others," she says. Those "others" are small business, young entrepreneurs, business professionals, or economic development efforts that attract jobs and decrease poverty.

In 2019, Carolyn was named the first female Distinguished Citizen of Year for the Chickasaw Boy Scouts Council. She was inducted into the Society of Entrepreneurs in 2016 and into the African American Hall of Fame in 2010. She received the 2016 Dr. Martin Luther King Legacy Award, the 2016 River City Links National Trends and Services Award, the 2014 Ruby Wharton Award for Business, the 2013 Legends Award from the Women's Foundation, and the 2012 Women of Achievement Award for Determination. In 2012, she was named as one of the 100 Women Who Inspired the Century by the University of Memphis Center for Women and African American Studies. She was also named 2012 Super Women in Business, 2011 University of Memphis Alumnus of the Year, and in 2009, Black Business Association named her business the Outstanding Woman-Owned Business and Business of the Year in 2008. These are only a few of the awards with which she and her businesses have been honored over the years.

Carolyn is married to Marino Hardy, and they are the proud parents of three wonderful children, Jennifer, Whitney, and Christopher.

GET REAL SMART

Tips to Get Started on Setting and Achieving Goals

1. Make Sure Your Goals are SMART: specific, measureable, attainable, relevant, and time specific. I also live my life by the KISS theory: keep it simple stupid. SMART is a simple guideline for setting goals anyone can follow.

Specific: Your goal is clearly defined. For example, "I want to lose weight" is vague. Instead, "I want to lose thirty pounds" is specific or "I want to graduate by 2019." List your specific goals; start with one or two.

_____

_____

_____

_____

_____

_____

_____

_____

_____

_____

Measurable: Quantify your goal so you know when it's achieved. Start by being specific as we discussed above. Losing weight is good but stating your specific goal will be more motivational. The thirty-pound weight loss or the year 2019 is measurable. What is your metric for your specific goal?

_____

_____

_____

_____

_____

_____

_____

_____

Attainable: Set a stretch goal that challenges you while making it realistic based upon your capabilities within your control. An unattainable goal may frustrate you and set you up for failure. Why is this a stretch goal?

_____

_____

_____

_____

_____

_____

_____

_____

_____

Relevant: Your goals help you achieve the life you deserve or achieve plans for your life. Therefore, it is important not only understand what your goals are but why they are important to you and your family. This will be your motivation to follow your plan. Why is this goal important to you and/or your family?

_____

_____

_____

_____

_____

_____

_____

Time Specific: Set a deadline (date) by which your goal will be achieved. A goal of losing thirty pounds without a date does not create a sense of urgency. Losing thirty pounds in eighteen months with interim weight loss at key milestones helps you monitor and measure your progress. By what date do you plan to accomplish this goal?

_____

_____

_____

_____

_____

_____

_____

_____

2. Set Milestones

The due date for a goal is typically far away. Many people put off starting until the first milestone approaches. Therefore, look at the project and set milestones based upon the accomplishment of anything significant. For example, losing weight may require a monthly weight loss goal since new habits are needed to stay on target. In the case of savings, if you want to save $100,000 and plan to save $2,000 per month, review the dollar amount saved monthly. This approach helps you monitor and measure your progress. Additionally, it helps you get back on target without significant time lapse if you do fall off the wagon for a little while. *Set time-specific milestones to break your goals into "bite size" to measure your progress along the way to achieving your goal.*

_____

_____

_____

3. Develop Action Steps to Reach Your Goals

List specific actions needed to reach big goals within the timeframe you decided on. In the case of weight loss, you may want to hire a personal trainer. Set a goal with the support of the trainer. Another key action could be to meet with a nutritionist to change your dietary habits. You may have a walking goal that gets increasingly aggressive over time. You may decide to run or walk a marathon after year one. These activities are all necessary to achieve the thirty-pound weight loss and create good habits to maintain your new weight. *List specific actions you will take to reach your goals.*

---

4. Put Your Actions into a Schedule

Develop a plan to get started. The first task will be the hardest as the first step but keep your eye on the prize (accomplishing your goal). It can be as simple as starting to walk each day. Next could be a call to a personal trainer and nutritionist to set up your first meetings to understand what is involved in the journey and lay to rest fears of the unknown. This first step will get you excited. Even if you start with baby steps, any action builds confidence and momentum. *List actions to get started. Remember, baby steps count to help you build confidence to gain momentum.*

_____

_____

_____

_____

_____

_____

5. Monitor Progress

Follow your schedule and do the daily tasks you've planned. Develop a plan that allows you to be consistent so your actions become new habits. This is critical to achieving your plan since you are trying to create a new norm for yourself. Your personal progress report will keep you motivated and create accountability to keep you on target. Remember: What gets measured gets done. I would recommend you maintain a log of your accomplishments and results. Set aside time every month to review your progress and make adjustments if necessary. *List your actual progress by month or other milestone that works for you.*

_____

_____

_____

_____

_____

Make a commitment to follow
these five SMART steps.

Remember: A goal without a plan
will remain an impossible dream.

Think about what you want to accomplish in life.
Then begin your journey to the life you deserve.
Before you know it, you will achieve
your impossible dream.

"Consult not your fears but your hopes and dreams. Think not about your frustrations but your unfulfilled potential. Concern yourself not with what you tried, and failed in, but with what it is still possible for you to do"
—Pope John Paul XXII

If you enjoyed *The Impossible Turned Possible*, Carolyn Chism Hardy is the author of two other amazing books. Please take a minute to read this brief introduction to each book. They will provide great advice to guide you on your journey to achieve the life you deserve.

Good Luck!

LOOK UP—
FIVE PRINCIPLES OF
INTENTIONAL LEADERSHIP

Carolyn Chism Hardy

Writing *Look Up* was a labor of love. *Look Up* was my first book, which has received rave reviews from readers who attest to the value of its advice.

Notes are my companions. I write them all the time. When I have something I want to research further, I hear an interesting quote or I have an idea for a new business deal, I open my notepad and start writing. Over the years, I have filled thousands of pages with lessons learned and great ideas. Although I graduated from college years ago, these notes are a record of my continued education. I have been on a lifelong odyssey of growth and discovery. This book is a peek into my journey.

There is inherent value in learning from the path another has taken. These notes are the foundation for the guidance offered in this book. You hold in your hands a collection of golden nuggets of knowledge I learned along the way. Many were taught to me by mentors like my mother; Dick Jirsa, former CFO of Smucker's; Bob Morrison, the COO of Smucker's; and countless others. I learned many other lessons the hard way through trial and error.

Leaders are like lighthouses. They are aware people look up to them for guidance. They light the way so others may reach their destination safely. Leaders offer guidance to buffer those who come after them. They keep them from hitting the rocks that are surely on their paths. They stand firm in their position and confident in their actions. This book will help you navigate away from the rocks and steer you into calmer waters.

The five principles in *Look Up* will be your lighthouse. The first principle is, "Plan Your Destiny" which helps the reader explore Know Your Why, Balance, and Don't Eat Excuses for Breakfast. The second principle is, "Make the Right Impression" which explores Know Your Worth, Stand Out, and Don't Let Bad News Age. The third principle is "Build Relationships" which discusses Understand Personalities, Don't Leave Dead Bodies and Never Let a Good Problem Go to Waste. The fourth principle is "Be the Change You Wish to See", which takes you through a journey of Use Your Education & Lean on Common Sense, Be Transparent and Become the Pro. The fifth principle is "Keep Calm and Carry On" which shares with the reader how to Be Prepared, Lead by Example and Always Pursue Growth.

Many people choose to ignore great advice. Some want to figure things out on their own. It's a lonely road for those who believe they don't need help. Those who can't master the principles in this book may never reach their destination.

During my career, discrimination towards my race and gender was commonplace. I had to endure prejudices that were unjust and unfair while maintaining my composure and work ethic. Overcoming obstacles that seemed insurmountable was critical to my success. I persevered because others who went before me showed me it was possible.

A great leader knows someone is always looking to them to be a role model, to motivate and lead the way. A French philosopher, Bernard of Chartres, once said, "We stand on the shoulders of giants." Almost 900 years later, his words still stand true. I stood on the shoulders of my mother. She passed along her wisdom and enabled me to benefit from the life she lived. I hope to do the same for you.

I hope anyone interested in rising to the challenge of leadership or entrepreneurialism will find guidance in the lessons I learned and the notes I took along the way.

Read this book, master the principles and remember to always, "Look Up." You are one of the giants on which the future depends.

STEP OUT–
BOLD MOVES FOR
BUSINESS GROWTH
Carolyn Chism Hardy

S *tep Out: Bold Moves for Business Growth* is Carolyn Chism Hardy's second book. As a serial entrepreneur and trailblazer, learning about business and winning started at an early age. *Step Out* shares early experiences of winning and losing playing marbles, the value of a sales pitch selling greeting cards before applying for her first retail job at the age of twelve. She has owned a major brewery, grain export company, electrical and mechanical supply company, beverage brand as well as commercial real estate.

Step Out shares how business challenges can be solved by experience and growth. Get ready to be captivated with real life stories that will build your confidence to believe in your ability to re-imagine your business. The reader will experience instant revelations as Step Out provides simple solutions to complex problems that has stalled their business success and growth.

Do you dare to begin the journey? Do you have what it takes to *Step Out* of your normal game? Are you afraid to grow but equally afraid to fail? Do you fear that growth will cause you to fail? Are you managing your business or is your business managing you?

Step Out is based upon forty years of professional and business ownership experience. What does it take to succeed and win in business?

- *Step Out* understands that work smarter not harder is a myth. Success requires working both smart and hard. The reality is the workday begins and ends when the customer needs are met in a timely manner. Remember Customer Service is a competitive advantage or disadvantage. *Step Out* will help you create competitive advantages.

- Public relation (PR) is key to business success and survival. Who should you communicate with, who is your target audience, when should you communicate and who is on your communication team. Effective PR is the difference between maintaining your hard-earned reputation and losing it in a flash.

- *Step Out* emphasizes that bold moves require risk taking. The mature risk taker calculates the risks associated with the opportunity. Observer may believe you are a fool or naive but bold moves executed effectively are required to transform your business.

- *Step Out* demonstrates that creativity and out of the box thinking is not just for someone else's business but is required in every business to survive then thrive. Step Out will help you jump-start your creative thinking to develop your plan for growth.

- *Step Out* shows the reader that mentors are not limited to the well-connected but necessary to gain external support to level the playing field. Learn who makes the best mentors, the mentor's roles and how to be a mentor or mentee.

- *Step Out* discusses the business owner's number one constraint to growth; insufficient working capital. Funding handcuffs most businesses. *Step Out* will help you create new ideas to gain funding from unusual sources.

Step Out's practical business processes introduces fresh ideas while connecting their importance to challenge business owners to honestly access their business. It is not only lonely at the top, but business ownership is lonely. Owners shoulder responsibility for all business issues. During dark times, *Step Out* will be the go-to companion when there is no one else around to listen or inspire. How?

- *Step Out* discusses specific business topics and provides creative concepts to teach the business owners best practices.
- *Step Out* shares personal stories to bring the concept to life while demonstrating this is not a concept but an industry best practice.
- *Step Out* concludes each chapter with a 'Call to Action' challenging business owners to be boldly honest in evaluating current practices and develop new best practices based upon your new learning.

Step Out teaches business owners when to challenge (or roll out) versus when to roll over. *Step Out* is the secret weapon to change business practices to win the growth game. Business owners need the courage to purchase the book and confidence to Step Out to start your transformational change. Her guidance is only as good as the actions you take while energized with fresh ideas and new strategies.